D1607214

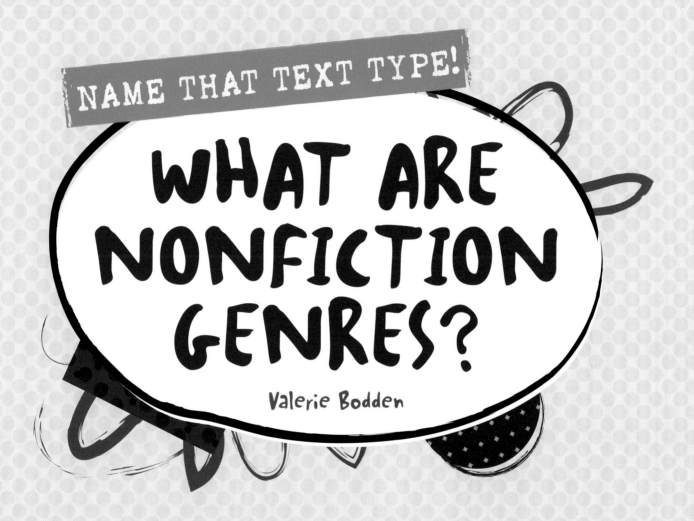

NAME THAT TEXT TYPE!

WHAT ARE NONFICTION GENRES?

Valerie Bodden

Lerner Publications Company • Minneapolis

Lerner Publications Company
A division of Lerner Publishing Group, Inc.
241 First Avenue North
Minneapolis, MN 55401 USA

For reading levels and more information, look up this title at www.lernerbooks.com.

Main body text set in Avenir LT Pro 15/21. Typeface provided by Linotype AG.

Library of Congress Cataloging-in-Publication Data

Bodden, Valerie.
    What are nonfiction genres? / by Valerie Bodden.
        pages   cm. — (Name that text type!)
    Includes index.
    ISBN 978–1–4677–3665–7 (lib. bdg. : alk. paper)
    ISBN 978–1–4677–4701–1 (eBook)
    1. Literary form—Juvenile literature. 2. Prose literature—Juvenile literature.
    I. Title.
    PN45.5.B63 2015
    808—dc23   2013040956

Manufactured in the United States of America
1 – BP – 7/15/14

Contents

Introduction:
THE REAL STORY

Do you like to know how things work? Do you wonder how life used to be? Want to find out more about a famous person? You can learn all these things from nonfiction.

The Daily News

NAL   VOL. 32 NO

50¢

OUSE P...

Nonfiction is writing about real life. It is made up of facts. Lots of books are nonfiction. Newspaper articles are nonfiction too. So are reports you write.

be harvested from exported technology is a matter of much debate. The National Energy Bureau published a monograph in 2006 outlining projections over the next ten years.

If everything goes according to plan, one out of every six Aboriginal could power their homes from PHART gas alone. Projections are even more optimistic in nations hardest hit by the war in Iraq such as Kurdistan where energy for transportation must be harvested from the emissions of farm animals.

In countries where petroleum is abundant, such as Iran, the reception

to the PHART initiative has bee... than enthusiastic. When intervi... the current President of Iran s... made a grotesque facial expr... and refused to comment any f... Later in an off-the-record exc... the president said he would... embrace PHART technology if... n't compromise air quality or... fere with his end-of-the-world... expected to be carried out by lo...

The nation's capitol shrouds the tempestuous fight within surrounding one of the most bizarre bills ever to reach the House floor.

...ued on

5

ountant Caught on Video- | DFL - GOP Runners Face Off

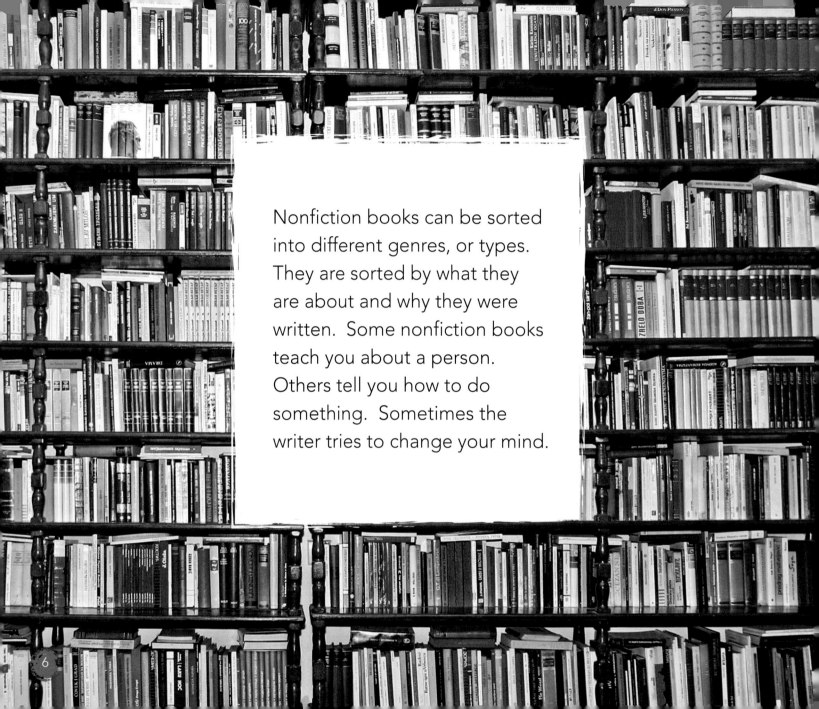

Nonfiction books can be sorted into different genres, or types. They are sorted by what they are about and why they were written. Some nonfiction books teach you about a person. Others tell you how to do something. Sometimes the writer tries to change your mind.

FINDING YOUR WAY

Nonfiction books make it easy to find what you need. Most have a table of contents. It is at the beginning of the book. It tells you the name of each chapter. It lists the chapter's first page. An index is at the end of the book. The index lists all the book's subjects. It also lists the pages that tell about those subjects. Some books have a glossary. The glossary gives the meanings of words you might not know.

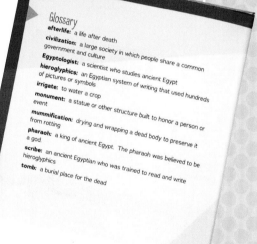

Glossary

afterlife: a life after death

civilization: a large society in which people share a common government and culture

Egyptologist: a scientist who studies ancient Egypt

hieroglyphics: an Egyptian system of writing that used hundreds of pictures or symbols

irrigate: to water a crop

monument: a statue or other structure built to honor a person or event

mummification: drying and wrapping a dead body to preserve it from rotting

pharaoh: a king of ancient Egypt. The pharaoh was believed to be a god.

scribe: an ancient Egyptian who was trained to read and write hieroglyphics

tomb: a burial place for the dead

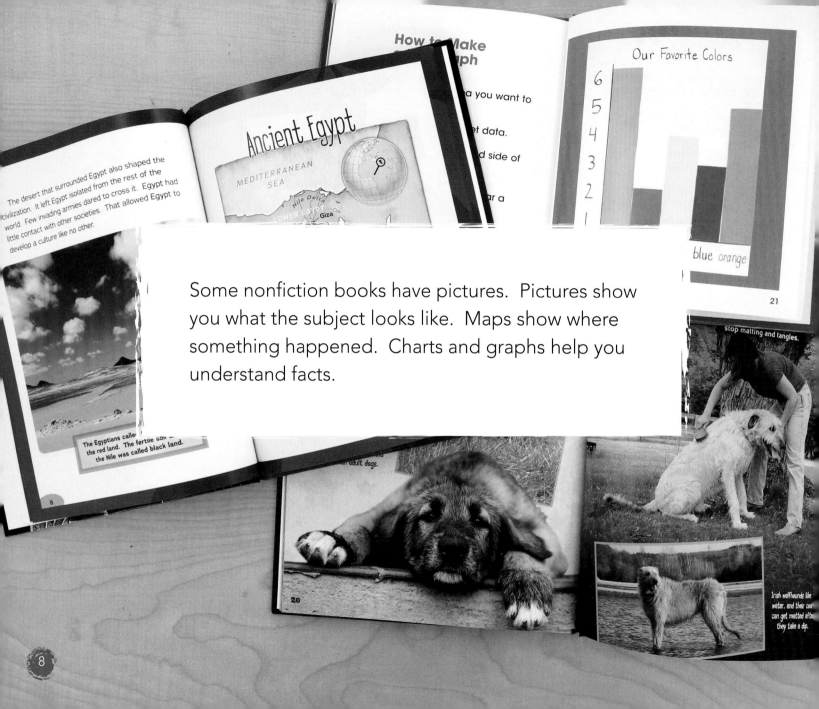

Some nonfiction books have pictures. Pictures show you what the subject looks like. Maps show where something happened. Charts and graphs help you understand facts.

The desert that surrounded Egypt also shaped the civilization. It left Egypt isolated from the rest of the world. Few invading armies dared to cross it. Egypt had little contact with other societies. That allowed Egypt to develop a culture like no other.

Ancient Egypt

MEDITERRANEAN SEA

Nile Delta

LOWER EGYPT

Giza

The Egyptians called the red land. The fertile soil the Nile was called black land.

How to Make ph

a you want to

t data.

d side of

r a

Our Favorite Colors

6
5
4
3
2
1

blue orange

21

stop matting and tangles.

adult dogs.

26

Irish wolfhounds like water, and their coa can get matted afte they take a dip.

8

Some nonfiction books are mostly facts. But other books are written like stories. Those books are called narrative nonfiction. Narrative nonfiction has characters and plots. It can be exciting. It makes you wonder what will happen next. The story might seem like fiction. But it is true!

Handle WITH Care

AN UNUSUAL BUTTERFLY JOURNEY

LOREE GRIFFIN BURNS

photographs by ELLEN HARASIMOWICZ

ALL ABOUT PEOPLE

Many nonfiction books are about people. A biography tells the story of a person's life. It is written by someone else. Many biographies are about famous people. A biography might be about a president. Or it could be about a sports star. A biography shows you what a person's life was like. The book might tell about the person's whole life. Or it might cover only part of someone's life. A biography makes you feel as if you know a person.

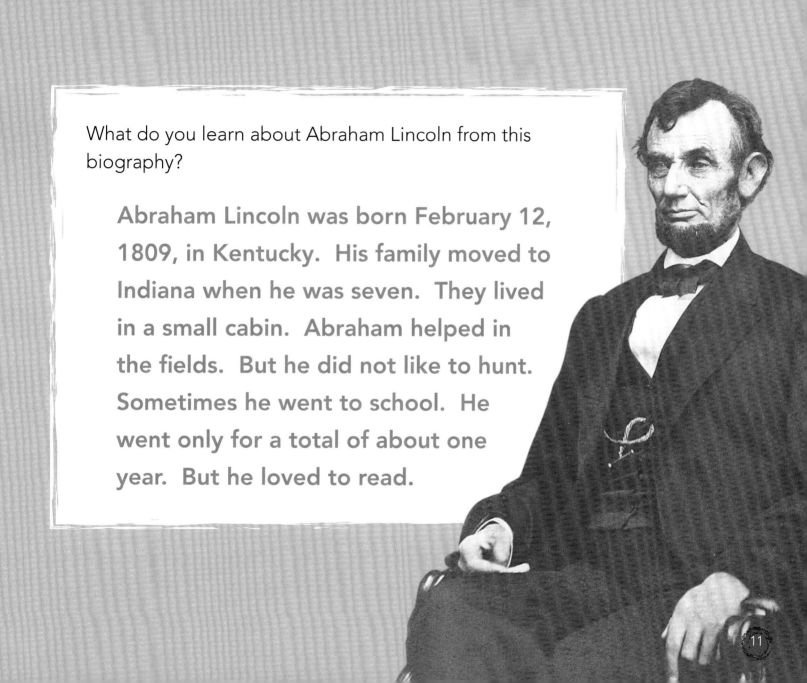

What do you learn about Abraham Lincoln from this biography?

Abraham Lincoln was born February 12, 1809, in Kentucky. His family moved to Indiana when he was seven. They lived in a small cabin. Abraham helped in the fields. But he did not like to hunt. Sometimes he went to school. He went only for a total of about one year. But he loved to read.

Some writers write books about themselves. These books are called autobiographies or memoirs. An autobiography tells about a person's whole life. A memoir usually tells about one part of someone's life. The memoir might be about her childhood. Or it could be about an adventure she had.

August.

me out of "gas mask" like tonite.
Fri.-4- Still on job, soft job under shade tree. "Stunt"

Sat. 10.

Sun. 11-

Mon.-12- Short drill this A.M. Went to range in P.M. to shoot "anti" Some fine sport. Came back + all stuff out in field. Slept in open.

August.

Tue.-13- Moved from Custoza. On baggage detail + rode to Valeggio. Pitch squad tents, but had to change

cross + "y"; makes life a little more interesting.
Aug. 15- Hatterinell. Batt. hikes thru Valeggio to river for movies. Caught hell for marching at ease

Autobiographies and memoirs can show you what a person thought and felt. So can journals. People usually write journals for themselves. They write about what is happening in their lives. Sometimes journals are made into books after the writer dies.

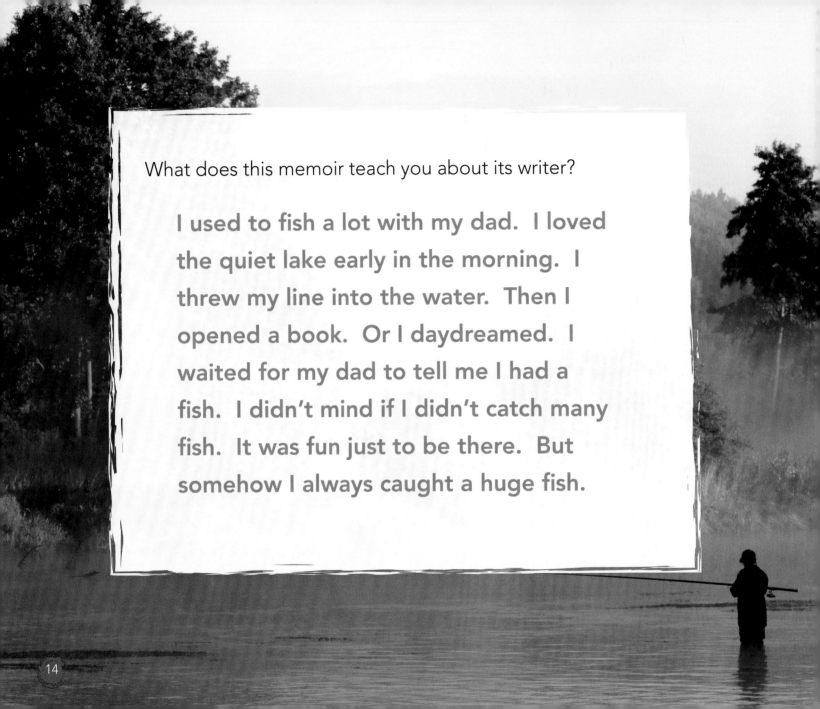

What does this memoir teach you about its writer?

I used to fish a lot with my dad. I loved
the quiet lake early in the morning. I
threw my line into the water. Then I
opened a book. Or I daydreamed. I
waited for my dad to tell me I had a
fish. I didn't mind if I didn't catch many
fish. It was fun just to be there. But
somehow I always caught a huge fish.

IN THE ACTION

Some nonfiction writing describes events. Things that happened recently are called current events. Newspaper articles tell about current events. News stories answer the questions who, what, where, when, and how. Sometimes they say why something happened.

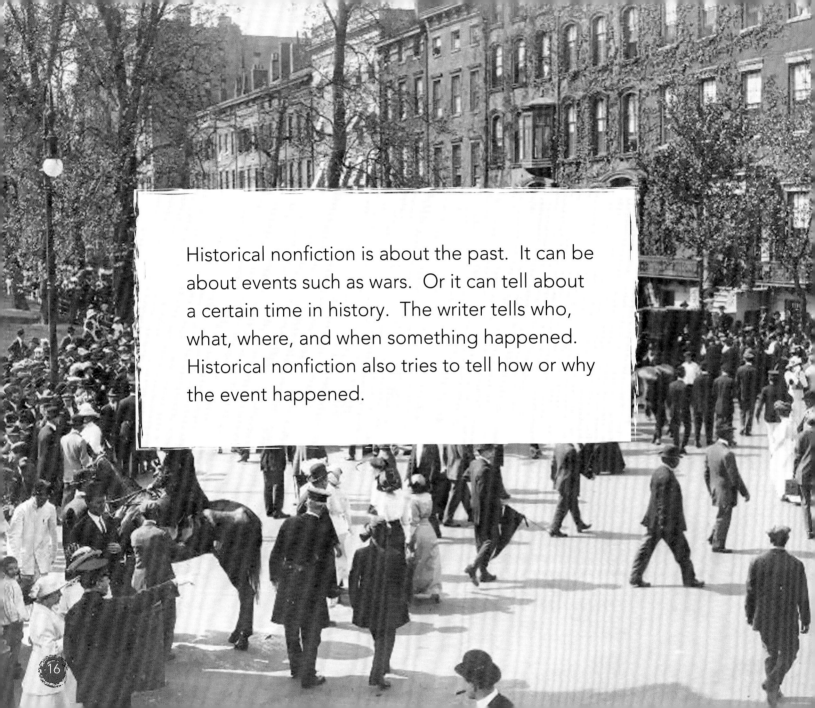

Historical nonfiction is about the past. It can be about events such as wars. Or it can tell about a certain time in history. The writer tells who, what, where, and when something happened. Historical nonfiction also tries to tell how or why the event happened.

This historical nonfiction is about people moving to New York. Why did they go? What was life like there?

In the early 1900s, most people lived on farms. But new machines had made farm work easier. Not as many people needed to farm. People looked for new ways to earn money. Millions moved to New York City. The city was crowded and noisy. It smelled bad. Garbage littered the streets. But there were new jobs. There were theaters to visit and trains and trolleys to ride.

True adventure books tell about exciting real-life events. Some explain how a person lived through danger. Others tell about sports events. True adventure books are often written as narrative nonfiction.

What makes this true adventure feel like a story?

Steven Callahan was alone in his boat. He was sailing across the Atlantic Ocean. Huge waves crashed over the boat. But Steven had seen worse weather. He had seen bigger waves. He thought his boat would be safe. He lay down in his bed. Suddenly he heard a loud crash. Water rushed into the boat. It was sinking. Steven had to get off!

TELL ME HOW

Some nonfiction books explain things. They can tell you all about an animal. Or they might show you how something works. They could deal with social studies, science, or art. These kinds of books teach you something new.

Look for all the facts about bees in this paragraph.

More than 20,000 kinds of bees live on Earth. All bees get food from flowers. The bees eat pollen and nectar. Most bees live alone. But honeybees live in colonies, or big groups. So do bumblebees.

Classic Pepperoni Pizza

Make your own version of this delicious, classic pizza. Serve it with some carrot sticks and apple slices to make

1. **Preheat** the oven

2. Prepare pizza doug
   it on the pan, as di
   dough recipe.

3. Use a grater to **gr**
   mozzarella cheese into a
   bowl or onto a plate.

spread the sauce on the pizza
over, but leave the edges of the
want to put more or less sauce
hick you like it.)

5. **Sprinkle** cheese on top.

6. **Place** pepperoni slices evenly on the pizza.

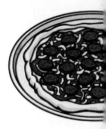

oven. Bake for 15 to 2
begin to turn a golde

of grated Parmesan c

How-to books tell you how to do something. They might teach you how to make a craft. Or they could tell you how to take care of a pet. Cookbooks are how-to books too. How-to books usually give step-by-step directions. Pictures might show each step.

Could you follow the steps of this how-to writing?

English muffin pizzas are easy to make.
First, split an English muffin in half.
Next, spread pizza sauce on each half.
Then top the sauce with shredded
cheese. Add your favorite toppings.
Put your pizza on a baking pan.
Finally, with an adult's help,
bake it at 350°F (177°C) for
about 10 minutes.

IT'S YOUR OPINION

Not all nonfiction is written to teach you. In persuasive nonfiction, writers tell you their opinions. They tell you the reasons for their opinions. They want you to agree with them. Or they want you to do something.

Do you agree with this writer's opinion about school uniforms?

All kids should wear school uniforms. Uniforms save parents money on clothes. They save kids time in choosing what to wear. And they keep kids from getting teased about their clothes. Tell your principal you want school uniforms!

Reviews are also based on opinions. A review is a writer's opinion about something. A review could be about a book or a movie. Or it might be about a play, a painting, or even a toy. The writer gives reasons for his or her opinion.

Did the writer of this review like the book? What reasons does she give for her opinion?

Santa Paws, Come Home is a great book. It is full of action as a dog named Santa Paws tries to escape from bad guys. Along the way, he has many adventures. I liked reading about life from a dog's point of view.

A WORLD OF FACTS

Reading nonfiction can teach you about the world around you. It can tell you about people and events from long ago. Or it can tell you what is going on now. It can be exciting, sad, funny, or scary. The best part is that it is all real!

The more nonfiction you read, the more you'll learn what genres you like. So pick up some nonfiction and learn something new!

Now You Do It

Try these activities to practice writing different kinds of nonfiction:

- A table of contents tells you the chapter names in a book. If you were going to write a book about yourself, what would you call the chapters? Write a table of contents. Then draw a picture for each chapter.

- A biography is a book about another person. Talk to a parent or a friend. Ask him or her questions. Where was she born? When? What else do you want to know about him? Then write a paragraph about the person.

- Think about something exciting that happened to you. Did you win a prize? Maybe you took a vacation. Who was there? What happened? Write a true adventure story about it. Tell it like a story. But make sure everything is true!

- How-to writing lists the steps you need to follow to do something. Think of something you do well. Do you make good peanut butter sandwiches? Maybe you can do a great cartwheel. List the steps you follow. Then be sure they are in the right order.

- What was the last book you read? Or think about a movie you watched. What happened? Did you like it? Write a review of the book or the movie. Explain why you did or didn't like it.

Glossary

autobiography: a true book about a person's life, written by that person

biography: a true book about a person's life, written by someone else

genre: a type of writing. A piece of writing's genre is based on its subject and why it was written.

glossary: a list of words and their meanings

index: a list of the subjects in a book and the pages that tell about those subjects

memoir: a book about part of a person's life, written by that person

narrative nonfiction: nonfiction that is written like a story, with characters and a plot

nonfiction: writing that is true, not made up

opinion: what someone thinks or believes

persuasive: able to make someone agree with an opinion or take a certain action

review: writing that tells what the writer thought of something, such as a book or movie

table of contents: a list of the chapters in a book and the pages they begin on

Further Information

Bodden, Valerie. *What Are Fiction Genres?* Minneapolis: Lerner Publications, 2015. Now that you know all about nonfiction, read this book to find out how fiction genres are different from other kinds of writing.

Fishman, Jon M. *Brittney Griner.* Minneapolis: Lerner Publications, 2014. Check out this biography of WNBA star Brittney Griner to see how to write about a person.

Fun English Games: Writing
http://www.funenglishgames.com/topics/writing.html
Try the games and activities on this site to practice and learn about different kinds of writing.

Hanlon, Abby. *Ralph Tells a Story.* New York: Marshall Cavendish Children, 2012. Follow along with Ralph as he struggles and finally manages to write a nonfiction story.

Pelleschi, Andrea. *Neil and Nan Build Narrative Nonfiction.* Chicago: Norwood House Press, 2014. Join Neil and Nan as they learn how to write nonfiction that sounds like a story.

LERNER
SOURCE

Expand learning beyond the printed book. Download free, complementary educational resources for this book from our website, www.lerneresource.com.

Index

Photo Acknowledgments

© Berezina/Shutterstock.com, p. 2, 30, 31, 32; © Quang Ho/Shutterstock.com, p. 4; © James Steidl/iStock/Thinkstock, p. 5; © Marko Beric/Hemera/Thinkstock, p. 6; © Lerner Publishing Group, Inc., p. 7, 8, 9, 10, 22; Library of Congress , p. 11, 16; © Christophe Testi/Thinkstock, p. 12 (pencil); © kiddy0265/iStock/Thinkstock, p. 12 (notebook); © TSpider/Shutterstock.com, p. 14; © broken3/iStock/Thinkstock, p. 15; © Gary Nash/iStock/Thinkstock, p. 17; © Matt Benoit/iStock/Thinkstock, p. 18; © Oskari Porkka/iStock/Thinkstock, p. 19; © Irina Kozhemyakina/iStock/Thinkstock, p. 20; © Dimitiy Smaglov/iStock/Thinkstock, p. 21; © Juanmonino/istock/Thinkstock, p. 23; © James Steidl/Thinkstock, p. 24; © Haze McElhenny/iStock/Thinkstock, p. 25; © noririn/iStock/Thinkstock, p. 26; © stoupa/iStock/Thinkstock, p. 27; © damircudic/Collection/Thinkstock, p. 28 © Photoraidz/Shutterstock.com, p. 29

Front Cover: © Lerner Publishing Group (book spreads); © robert_s/Shutterstock.com (ipad).